LEADERS OF
ANCIENT GREECE

SOLON

The Lawmaker
of Athens

LEADERS OF ANCIENT GREECE

SOLON

The Lawmaker of Athens

Bernard Randall

the rosen publishing group's
rosen
central

Published in 2004 by The Rosen Publishing Group, Inc.
29 East 21st Street, New York, NY 10010

First Edition

Library of Congress Cataloging-in-Publication Data

Randall, Bernard.
Solon : the lawmaker of Athens / Bernard Randall.
   p. cm. — (Leaders of ancient Greece)
Includes bibliographical references and index.
ISBN 0-8239-3829-8
1. Solon, ca. 630–ca. 560 B.C. 2. Athens (Greece)—Politics
and government. 3. Statesmen—Greece—Biography.
I. Title. II. Series.
DF224.S7 R26 2003
938'.502'092—dc21

(Solon)
NoB

2002004584

Manufactured in the United States of America

Contents

GREECE AT THE TIME OF SOLON

BLACK SEA

MACEDONIA

THRACE

AEGEAN SEA

● Sigeum

● Acanthus

● Phocaea

● Ephesus

● Chalcis
● Eritrea

Delphi ● Thebes ●

● Miletus

● Athens

● Corinth

PELOPONNESE

● Halicarnassus

Olympia ● Argos

● Sparta

IONIAN SEA

CRETE

MEDITERRANEAN SEA

ATHENS BEFORE SOLON

CHAPTER 1

2

3

4

More than 2,500 years ago, in 594 BC, a statesman named Solon changed forever the constitution of what was then an insignificant city in Greece—Athens. Years later, the Athenians came to refer to him as the Father of Democracy. Modern ideas of democracy and the rule of law come from the ancient Athenians. Yet scholars know very little about the life of this man to whom humanity owes so much. In fact, historians are certain of only a few of the things that Solon did to make democracy possible. A few lines of the poetry he wrote and some legends are all that survive. However, we can piece together, both from what we know about the times he lived in and from the effects of what he did, the remarkable achievements of Solon.

The goddess Athena, daughter of Zeus, warrior goddess, patroness of the arts, and protectress of the city of Athens. Athena was also considered the goddess of wisdom, since legend has it that she was born from Zeus's head.

THE NATURE OF GREECE

In ancient times, Greece was wherever Greeks lived. At the time of Solon, this included most of what is now Greece, most of southern Italy, the Aegean coast of Turkey, and the western and northern coasts of the Black Sea. All Greeks spoke a common language, although there were several distinct dialects. There was also a common culture, including religious beliefs.

Most Greeks belonged to a *polis*, or city-state, and each polis had its own unique political arrangements. At any time there might be ten to twenty poleis (the plural of polis) that had influence outside their own territories, but there would be many hundreds of smaller poleis. Some of these smaller poleis cooperated by forming leagues or confederacies between themselves or with the larger or more powerful poleis.

The Greeks were usually fiercely loyal to their poleis and would see themselves as citizens of Athens, or Corinth, or Sparta, and the like, before they thought of themselves as Greeks. Many would consider exile from their polis as a fate little better than death.

In ancient Greece, each polis was an independent state, even if it had only a few thousand inhabitants. Before the Greeks invented democracy, the aristocracy ran most poleis. Aristocrats were people who owned enough land to be able to exchange the produce from their farms for luxury items, horses, or weapons. Swords were very expensive, and only a few people could afford them. The Greeks believed that the only people who should have power in a polis were those who were able to fight to defend it against its enemies. Because only the wealthy could afford weapons, only the rich had power. Of those who were not aristocrats, most were peasant farmers whose land provided enough food for themselves and their families. The peasants were mostly loyal to the aristocrats because the rich were able to protect the polis from its enemies. There were also a few traders and artisans, who provided services to others.

An important characteristic of the aristo-cratic families was that they could trace their genealogy back many generations. Often they believed that they were descended from the gods. These families believed that they had always been rich and always owned lots of land.

THE GOVERNMENT OF ATHENS

In Athens, the aristocrats, sitting in a council known as the Areopagus, elected magistrates each year. It is thought that the most senior members of each family were members of the Areopagus. The title of the most important magistrate was *archon*, who was the head of state. There was also the *polemarch*, who commanded the army. There were seven other magistrates: the "king archon," who had mostly religious responsibilities, and six "decision recorders," who kept a record of all the judgments made by the magistrates and various other lesser officials. For all except the polemarch, their main job was to act as judges in the law courts. The aristocrats elected only each other, so the courts would always favor the aristocrats if they had to decide between themselves and the peasants. What made it even harder for peasants to get justice was that the Athenians did not write down the *nomoi* [singular: *nomos*], the customs or laws. This meant that it was impossible to check whether a judge's decision was right or not. The judge would take into account his own opinion, as well as the decisions of other judges in the past. The Athenians did write down the decisions of judges, but since no two cases would ever be exactly the same, a judge did not need to take much notice of them. Having written records would have been of little help

A Greek vase painting showing a sacrificial bull being led to the altar. The sacrifice of animals to the gods was a central element in Greek religion.

to the peasants anyway, since most were probably illiterate. It would be easy for a greedy judge to take someone's land.

Toward the end of the seventh century BC, trade between Greece and the rest of the Mediterranean world had significantly increased. Many Athenian merchants became very rich and were able to buy farms around Athens, in the region known as Attica. Such merchants could now afford to pay for weapons and therefore expected a share in power. However, the aristocrats did not allow the

A bowl made in ancient Athens

merchants to join the aristocracy, which was composed of a small group of families. The aristocrats did not elect the newly rich as magistrates. Even though the newly rich might have had more wealth than the aristocrats, they were still at a disadvantage when it came to legal and political matters. Their only chance of winning a case in the courts would have been by bribing the magistrate who was acting as a judge. It is easy to see how this situation made the newly rich unhappy. As time went by, more and more merchants gained wealth. The only

The ruins of Eleuthe-
rai, one of several
forts that encircled
and protected Athens

way they could gain power was to take it by force. In many Greek poleis during the seventh century BC, a tyrant, who had the support of the newly rich, seized power.

THE ATTEMPTED TYRANNY OF KYLON

Around 632 BC, Kylon attempted to seize power at Athens as a tyrant. An aristocrat, he was married to the daughter of Theagenes, the tyrant of Megara, a polis neighboring Athens and one of her fiercest enemies.

Kylon had won an event in the Olympic Games in 636 BC. Olympic victors were the celebrities of ancient Greece. The Greeks held state dinners in honor of such athletes and gave them the best seats at religious festivals. The ancient Olympic Games were different in many ways from the games played today. In ancient times, far fewer events were held, only the winner of an event received recognition, and the games were always held in the same location. Although there were other competitions, the Olympic Games were the most prestigious. Competitors came from all over the Greek world to participate. Kylon attempted to use his prestige as a victorious athlete to start a political career.

Kylon came to Athens with a band of armed supporters and friends from Megara, and they seized control of the Acropolis, the hill in the center of the city. Megakles, an aristocrat who was archon that year, brought together the people of Athens and besieged Kylon. Although the aristocrats were unpopular, Kylon had made a mistake. The ordinary people of Athens were not yet so unhappy that they would allow someone who had joined forces with their enemy to control their polis.

Kylon managed to escape secretly, but his supporters were not so lucky. Their food ran out, and they took sanctuary in one of the temples. Megakles broke the deadlock by persuading them to come out in exchange for the promise of a fair trial. As they were coming out of the temple, Megakles and his supporters attacked and murdered them. Megakles died soon afterward, but the Athenians never forgot this crime. Historians presume that Kylon never returned to Athens, but his family was still there. There was increasing tension between the families of Megakles and Kylon, and eventually the children of Megakles were put on trial for sacrilege and sent into exile. However, they returned a few years later when the archon was more friendly to them. For the next 200 years, the descendants of Megakles were exiled whenever their political enemies were in power, and they were recalled when their friends were in control.

WHAT WAS TYRANNY?

Although the Greeks invented democracy, not all poleis used the system. Up to the seventh century BC, most poleis were run by aristocrats who ruled for their own benefits. Normally there was a balance of power, and the different families would take turns holding the magistracies. However, an aristocrat who became more powerful than the others, because of popular support, might take control and rule as an individual with supreme power. Such an individual ruler was called a tyrant. Usually the tyrant became powerful enough to take control because of support from the newly rich merchant class.

A vase painting depicting the grape harvest

The newly rich in a polis had no political rights, and they would support anyone who promised to make their lives better. If a tyrant was ruling the polis, no one else had real political power. Although the tyrant might keep the old system of magistrates, he would ensure that only his friends and supporters were chosen. The lives of the newly rich were better because under a tyrant they received equal treatment with the aristocrats. Because they had supported the tyrant, he would tend to favor their interests. For example, a tyrant might try to make trading easier for those he favored.

Another feature of Greek tyrants was that they supported each other. It was very common for one tyrant to be connected to another by marriage. A tyrant, for instance, might be married to the daughter of another. Sometimes, if a tyrant was threatened with revolution, other tyrants would send soldiers to help prevent it.

Although each polis was independent, when tyrants were in charge there were networks of alliances between them.

At some time or other in the history of almost every polis, a tyrant ruled it. Some poleis were ruled by a series of tyrants over hundreds of years, with sons inheriting power from their fathers. In others, after a while the people threw out the tyrant and set up a democracy. This was possible because the tyrants had already taken power away from the aristocrats.

Tyrants came to power with popular support. If, when a tyrant died, his son was not popular, the son would have to use force to keep control. It was often the sons or grandsons of the original tyrants who were thrown out in a revolution. The less popular the new tyrant was, the more brutal the regime had to be, and the more chance there was of a revolution.

The ruins at Olympia, where the first Olympic Games—then just a local festival—were held

Today, the word "tyrant" means a brutal dictator. But for the Greeks, this was not necessarily the case. A tyrant could be good or bad. The word "tyrant" applied more to the method of gaining power than to the style of rule once the tyrant achieved power. If one of the ancient Greek philosophers were alive today, he would think of the democratically elected leaders of the Western nations as tyrants. This is because they come to power with popular support. Except in exceptional circumstances, they keep power throughout their period of office, they rule (with advice) as individuals, and they are usually the commander in chief of the military. The president of the United States is not a brutal dictator, but he is a tyrant in the Greek sense of the word.

THE NOMOI OF DRAKON

Kylon had come close to overthrowing the aristocracy, and the rivalry between the families of Kylon and Megakles threatened to break out into violence at any time. This situation greatly worried the aristocrats. They did not wish to give anyone else a chance to exploit the unhappiness of the newly rich.

And so, in 621 BC, the aristocrats who ruled Athens decided to ask a man called Drakon to produce some nomoi, or laws, to keep peace and order.

We know nothing about what Drakon's nomoi were. Solon repealed all of the nomoi of Drakon, except for one about homicide, and the Athenians quickly forgot them. Legend tells us that they were very harsh. The English word "draconian," meaning very harsh, comes from his name. Athenians later said that Drakon gave the death penalty for most crimes, even stealing fruit. The story goes that when someone asked Drakon why this was, he answered that he thought that minor crimes deserved death, and he could think of no worse punishment for serious ones.

Whatever they were really like, the nomoi of Drakon certainly did not keep the peace. The newly rich continued to be unhappy at their lack of political power, and as their numbers increased, they must have seemed more threatening than ever. Their rivalry with the aristocrats showed no signs of abating. To make matters worse, by the end of the seventh century BC a new problem had appeared. This was the problem of debt.

ECONOMIC PROBLEMS

Although the precise reasons are unknown today, many peasant farmers in Solon's time got themselves into debt. Traditionally, farmers must live on credit until they can sell their harvests. Perhaps the harvest was bad several years in a row. Or, possibly, the aristocrats who ran the courts became greedy when they saw the increased wealth of the newly rich and began to make life more difficult for the peasants through taxation. Or, it could be that the big farms of the aristocrats produced extra grain, and its price fell. This would mean that poorer farmers needed more land to produce the same value of grain as in the past, and they could only get more land and the tools to work it by borrowing from the aristocrats.

An artist's reconstruction of an ancient Greek warship, which employed both a sail and oars

The problem for the peasants was that if they were unable to repay their loans by the deadline, their creditors could force them and their families into slavery. As slaves, they were subject to the whims of their owners, who could either keep them or sell them to other people. Sometimes the purchasers of these newly enslaved people were foreigners, and they transported their new slaves to another part of Greece or the Mediterranean. It seems that many peasants who were about to become slaves because of debt left Athens and went to live abroad voluntarily. It was better for them to be free than enslaved, wherever they had to live.

Many poor Athenian farmers became *hektemoroi*, or tenant farmers. The name means "sixth-parters." Scholars are uncertain whether this indicated that the farmers paid one-sixth of their produce to a landowner as rent, or that they kept one-sixth of their produce as pay. If they paid one-sixth, then the five-sixths they kept seems to be plenty, and their lives would not have been very difficult. If the farmers kept only one-sixth, that amount seems much too little to live on. Modern historians cannot agree on this. Perhaps if peasants paid one-sixth, it was not one-sixth of their produce, but one-sixth of the value of their land, though we have no idea how that could be assessed. Or if they kept one-sixth, perhaps they only kept one-sixth of the grain but were able to keep all the other produce of their farms. Either of these situations would mean that life was hard but livable. What we are certain of is that the hektemoroi were unhappy about their status. They likely became hektemoroi because of some kind of debt. Once they were in this position, there was no way out. It was impossible for them to improve their status. The hektemoroi were regarded as little better than slaves. Thus, if they did not work hard enough for the landowners, it is possible that they actually became slaves.

SLAVERY

Various forms of slavery existed in the ancient world. The most common was chattel slavery. A chattel slave was the property of an individual ("chattel" is an old word for property). The owner could sell the slave at any time, and the slave had no legal rights. If an owner had a number of chattel slaves, both male and female, it was not unusual for the slaves to form relationships and have children. However, the owner could sell one or both parents, or any of the children, and split up the family. The type of work done could range from household duties or running the owner's shop to working on a farm or in a mine.

Chattel slaves could be acquired in various ways. After military victories, for example, captives were often sold as slaves. Pirates might take prisoners from coastal settlements and enslave them. The slave trade thrived throughout the Mediterranean, with slave-traders shipping their cargoes from one region to another. Slaves were usually not indigenous to the land in which they were forced to work. Any children of slaves were slaves themselves, so slaves could be obtained by a deliberate breeding program as well.

Another type of slavery occurred when one polis conquered another. The victors forced the entire defeated population to work for them, without moving them from their farms. These slaves were owned by the polis and could be sold only by the polis, not by individuals. This type of slavery did not exist in Athens.

In addition, the word "slave" could indicate anyone who was forced to work for someone else because of legal obligations. This kind of "slave" could not be sold. In contrast, a hired laborer had to work to get food but was not forced to do so and could choose to starve instead. This use of the word "slave" indicates someone who did not have free choices in everything but who was not a slave in the strictest sense.

In the time of Solon, only the wealthy could afford to own slaves, and most productive work was still performed by those who were free. It was only later that Athens became wealthy enough for slave ownership to be common. Slavery was an accepted part of life, but it probably did not make much difference in most people's lives—at least, that is, until they found themselves in debt and risked becoming enslaved.

THE CHANGE TO COINAGE

The whole economy of the Mediterranean world was also beginning to change at this time. In what is now modern Turkey, coins were invented around 630 BC. Today, it is hard to imagine a world without money. But then it was a new invention, and it took time for people to get used to the idea. Farmers had always exchanged part of their crops for goods that they could not grow or make for

A sixth-century BC marble head of Zeus, father of the Greek gods

themselves. If they needed iron to make a plough, they could swap grain for it. They could easily see how the labor they put into their crops could be converted into goods. As such, it took some time for people to accept that a coin, a small disk of silver, could be accepted as payment and later traded for a certain amount of goods, such as olive oil. Since the aristocrats controlled the production of coins, they were able to decide how much the coins were worth. For the first time it was possible to have banks. It was easier to store wealth because coins did not rot and perish like grain. Aristocrats had always exchanged precious metals for luxury items, so the change was not so great for them. But it was a new experience for the peasant farmers to deal with objects that had no practical use to them.

The Athenians did not produce their own coins until around 575 BC, and we do not know how much impact foreign currency had on the Athenian economy before Solon's reforms in 594 BC. But this new invention would change the world forever. The aristocrats were in a position to take advantage of the peasants, as they could demand payment for debts in currency, which was always scarce with poor farmers. Then, the aristocrats could enslave the peasants when payments could not be made. The new style of doing business could only have made the situation worse.

One way or another, the people of Athens were unhappy. The aristocrats feared someone might try to become a tyrant. Kylon had come close, and the new laws of Drakon had not helped. Everyone else had good reason to want change. The newly rich were angry because they had no share of political power. Peasant farmers were suffering from debt and the danger of being made into slaves. The hektemoroi were unhappy because of their hard lives and lack of freedom. If the situation continued, the polis might descend into chaos. So in 594 BC, the Athenians turned to Solon. The aristocrats elected him archon, giving him complete power to change everything as long as he would prevent the crisis they feared.

SOLON IS ELECTED ARCHON

The details of Solon's early life are sketchy. His father was Exekestides, and his mother, whose name is unknown today, was related to Peisistratos (who is discussed later). Historians estimate that Solon was born around 640 BC and died in 561 BC or a little later, at the age of eighty.

Solon's family was in the aristocracy, but it was not one of the richest. The education of aristocratic boys consisted of learning to read and write, as well as some kind of musical training, most likely singing and playing the lyre. Solon would have studied Homer, perhaps even memorizing his poems. The verse of Homer, according to aristocratic Greeks in Solon's time, contained everything that a respectable Greek needed to know about religion and proper behavior. Boys would have participated in some physical education as well. Athletics and wrestling were considered suitable for aristocratic young men. In his late teens and early twenties, Solon may well have received some basic military training, too.

The legends about Solon say that his father, Exekestides, was very generous to the needy, so generous in fact that there was very little left for Solon to inherit when his father died. As a result, Solon became a merchant, sailing around the Mediterranean to make a living. In that era, such activities were not undertaken by "respectable" aristocrats. For the Greeks, the only respectable source of income for an aristocrat was earned from the land. However, Solon's choices were limited, so he set off to make his fortune. The situation proved advantageous for Solon. During his travels, he saw the different ways that other poleis and non-Greek states organized their constitutions. This experience would have helped him a great deal when he came to change the Athenian constitution.

Many stories are told about Solon's travels, and it is safe to say that they are most likely untrue. There was a tendency in the ancient world to attach an interesting story to anyone famous, and Solon was very famous. He was one of the Seven Sages of the Greeks. The Seven

An idealized sculpture of the blind poet Homer. This marble bust is from the Roman period, in the second century BC, although Homer is supposed to have lived during the eighth century BC.

Sages were men who were famous for their wisdom, and most were statesmen of one polis or another. One of the sages, Thales of Miletus, is often regarded as the first philosopher in the Western tradition. Many stories were told about the sages, including little fables or parables, which illustrated points of moral behavior. Which sage was the hero of a story would depend on who was telling it. An Athenian would tell a story about Solon, whereas someone from Miletus might tell the same story about Thales. In fact, the names of the Seven Sages varied throughout the Greek world. Each region had its own idea about who was one of the seven. In all, twenty-two different people were said to be one of the Seven Sages. However, Solon was recognized universally. Many famous sayings are attributed to the Seven Sages. Two of the best remembered today are "Know yourself" and "Nothing to excess." Solon had a high reputation for wisdom in the ancient world after his own time, which may reflect a similarly high reputation in his own day.

WHY SOLON WAS ELECTED

One episode that shows the profile Solon had in Athenian public life before he was elected archon was the capture of the island of Salamis, which lies just off the coast of Attica, in the territory of Athens. Its strategic location allowed control of access to the harbors of Athens. The Athenians seem to have fought a long war against Megara for control of Salamis. Megara was just along the coast of Athens, and Salamis was very close to the harbor of Megara. It is not known who originally owned the island, but certainly the Athenians believed that it ought to be theirs.

Sometime just after 600 BC, the Megarians managed to take control of Salamis so decisively that the Athenians decided to give up the fight. The Athenians went so far as to pass a law stating that anyone who proposed restarting the war for Salamis should be put to

A sixth-century BC relief carving of a man with his dog seated on a stool, from the Acropolis in Athens

death. It seems that Solon was unwilling to settle for this. So he had his family tell people that he had gone mad. Then one day he rushed into the marketplace. A big crowd gathered to find out what this man, whom they believed to be mad, would do. Solon recited a poem he had composed, which began:

> As my own herald I have come from lovely
> Salamis,
> Having composed ordered words, a song
> instead of a speech.

And he went on to urge the Athenians:

> Let us go to Salamis, fight for that lovely
> island
> And fling off our bitter disgrace.

The Athenians were so moved by Solon's poem that they changed the law again and decided to make another attempt to capture Salamis. The story seems fanciful, but there is no reason to doubt the authenticity of the poem. Accordingly, the story may be essentially true as well.

Under the leadership of Solon, the Athenians managed to recapture Salamis.

A small sixth-century BC statue of a farmer behind his plow and oxen

Exactly how this was done is unknown because the stories are rather confused. However, one version claims that Solon called for 500 volunteers and promised them that they would govern the island if they captured it. If this is what happened, then it reveals how bad conditions were for most Athenians. The prospect of having political rights in Athens itself must have seemed so low that these volunteers were willing to risk their lives and then to move themselves and their families across the water to an island that would possibly be a battlefield again. Perhaps it was the strength of desire for political rights that gave these volunteers the incentive to win the battle for Salamis. Although there was more fighting to come, Salamis did end up as part of Athenian territory. Years later, a statue of Solon was erected in the main town on the island, and the people of Salamis could point out a temple to Ares, the god of war, which they believed Solon had built. There was even a legend that after Solon's death, his ashes were sprinkled over the island. The advice Solon gave in the Salamis situation was one crucial factor in the Athenians' decision to appoint him archon.

After the victory at Salamis, it seems that Solon may have been chosen as an ambassador for Athens. Following that, he gave advice to the Greeks to ensure the independence of the oracle at Delphi. An oracle, according to the Greeks, was someone who could receive messages directly from the gods. The temple of the Delphic Oracle was the most sacred site in Greece, and the Amphiktyonic League had been established to protect it. The Amphiktyonic League was a group of poleis, including Athens, that had sworn to cooperate to protect the sacredness of Delphi. They would send ambassadors to twice yearly meetings.

At one of these meetings, league members discussed what to do about the polis of Krisa,

The temple of Apollo at Delphi, where the Greeks came to ask the oracle about their fates

which was making life difficult for people visiting the oracle. Krisa controlled the road to Delphi and was forcing people to pay tolls. At the meeting of the league, Solon advised the Greeks that they could not allow themselves to be prevented from using the oracle freely and that they should go to war to guarantee its freedom. They took his advice, and Krisa was destroyed in what was called a "sacred war." Solon had come to the attention of the Athenians in very dramatic ways, and his advice had worked to their advantage. As such, it was logical that the aristocrats looked to him when they finally decided to do something about the political crisis facing Athens.

Solon must have seemed a good choice for more general reasons as well. He was an aristocrat, but he was not from an extremely rich family. This meant two things. First, there would be no reason for other aristocrats to

An overview of the ruins at Delphi. Treasuries were built near many of the religious sanctuaries to display the offerings of particular city-states.

be jealous of his position. The most influential families were the richest, and no doubt the richest few families would be in constant competition to get their own members into the magistracies. Solon came from outside this circle of competing families, and therefore he would not upset the balance too much. Second, and just as important, Solon was politically prominent by virtue of the good advice he had been giving and not simply by his aristocratic background. As a result, the poorer sections of Athenian society could trust him to be fair to them. In addition, the fact that Solon had spent time as a merchant must have made him an acceptable mediator to the newly rich, who had made most of their money through trade.

And, of course, there were Solon's poems. It seems that Solon gave recitals of his poetry, in which he commented on the state of affairs in Athens. No doubt

A Greek vase depicting a struggle between two boxers

Solon produced poetry partly because he enjoyed it but also because he lived in a society that valued the spoken word. Although most Athenians could probably read a little, few would have been able to write well. Thus, almost all communication had to be spoken. In addition, poetry is easier to remember than prose, so it is natural to use this method if the purpose is to give people something to go away with and discuss. The Greek world had a long tradition of using poetry to give advice. The Greeks would look in the works of Homer, the earliest Greek poet, for advice on subjects like religion and fighting wars. Another of the earliest Greek poets, Hesiod, wrote about religion and farming.

It is unknown whether Solon wrote his poems because he hoped to get the position of archon, or whether he simply wanted to advise the Athenians about social issues. His concern for Athens seems genuine. One of his poems begins:

> I am aware, and pain lies heavy in my heart,
> That I watch the oldest Ionian state [Athens] sinking.

A sixth-century BC painting of a warrior with his shield and spear

There can be no doubt that Solon knew about the troubles facing Athens. And he seems to have blamed the wealthy in his poems:

> They are rich because they trust in unjust methods.

At the time Solon was elected, one of his phrases was going around Athens: "Equality creates no conflict." Apparently, the rich thought that he meant equality of opportunity, and the poor thought he meant equality of land ownership—sharing the land equally.

Solon was elected archon in 594 BC, with full power to reform the constitution however he thought best. The election was probably by a show of hands at a meeting of the Areopagus, the council of aristocrats. All sides thought that Solon would benefit them. The changes he made earned him the reputation, 200 years later, as the Father of Democracy.

SOLON'S REFORMS

As discussed earlier, one of the main problems facing Athens was debt. Solon's first order of action was to decree a broad cancellation of debts. The details of this action are sketchy today, but it came to be known by the name *seisachtheia*, which means the "shaking off of burdens." It is unlikely that Solon actually used the word himself, since it is in none of his surviving poetry, so the word was probably first used by later writers.

One of the stories told about Solon is that just before he passed his law canceling debts, he mentioned his plans to some aristocratic friends. They took the opportunity to borrow large amounts of money, knowing that they would not have to repay it. However, when people realized what had happened, Solon's friends were disgraced. This nearly ruined Solon's political career because he had leaked the information. But Solon was able to demonstrate that he, too, had lost from uncollected debts. It is likely that the allegations against him were false and were just devised by someone who was unhappy with Solon's cancellation of debt or his other reforms. The story does reveal that the cancellation likely applied to all debts, and not just those of a selected few, or to a certain amount of someone's overall debt. However, canceling all debt was an extremely radical thing to do, so there remains some doubt as to whether that is actually what Solon did.

Another important problem that deeply concerned the poorest farmers was the threat of falling into slavery. Solon set free anyone who had been enslaved because of debt. He also brought home those who had been sold to foreigners and those who had gone into exile because of debt. His poetry provides evidence of this:

> I brought back to their divinely founded
>   home many Athenians
> Who had been sold abroad, either illegally
> Or legally, and those whom poverty had
>   driven away,

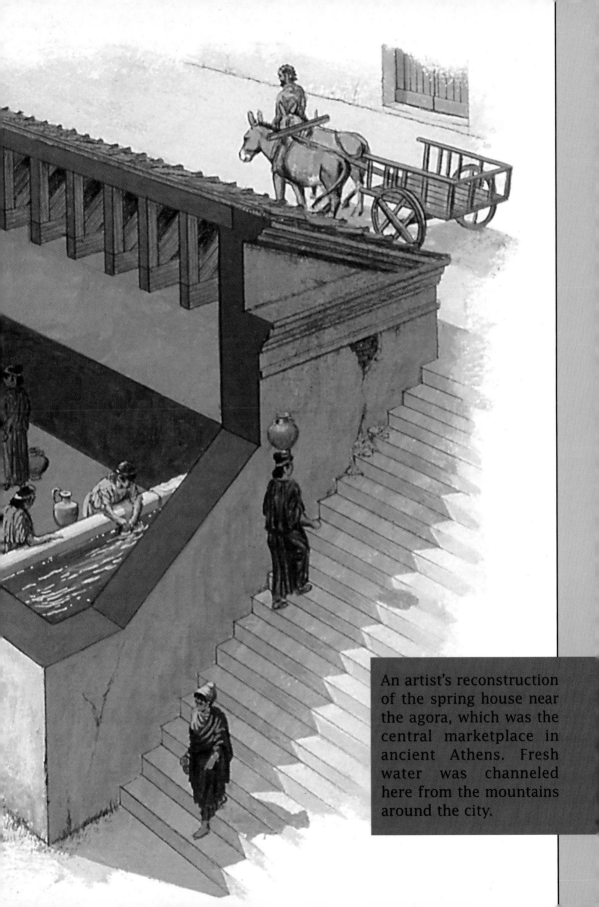

An artist's reconstruction of the spring house near the agora, which was the central marketplace in ancient Athens. Fresh water was channeled here from the mountains around the city.

> And no longer spoke the Attic dialect
>   because of their exile.
> And I set free those who had been made
>   slaves
> Here at home, and feared their masters.

Again, the fact that slaves were released was effectively a complete cancellation of the debt for which they had been enslaved. The return of those who had gone into exile because they were unable to pay their debts also required the cancellation of those debts. Some aristocrats who sold people into slavery because of their debts had not always followed the nomoi, or law. They must have seized the land of peasants and sold the farmers into slavery without going through the earlier proper process.

No form of compensation for the debts that were cancelled could have been made because, at that time, Athens would not have had reserves of wealth to use for this purpose. Taxes were collected but only on a small scale, and only enough to pay for what was needed. No government treasury existed that might be tapped for compensation to the slaveholders. This created a problem in bringing home any

Athenians who had been sold to foreign owners. Their new owners were not Athenians, so no law passed by Solon could force them to give up their slaves. Someone would have to buy back the slaves. This could be done only by the Athenian aristocrats who had sold them initially. The profits from the sale of slaves now had to be used to buy back the slaves.

A horos, or boundary stone, indicating that the land it is on was purchased with a loan

Another aspect of the seisachtheia was the removal of *horoi* (stones used to mark the boundaries of land ownership). Solon wrote:

> From the black Earth I
> Pulled up the horoi that had been planted
>   everywhere,
> So what was formerly enslaved is now free.

Considerable debate exists among historians regarding what the removal of the horoi would achieve. The normal meaning of "horoi" is "boundary markers." It was considered a very serious religious offense to remove such markers, and simply removing boundaries would not do anything to help the peasant farmers. The other meaning of horos (the singular of horoi) is "mortgage stone," indicating that a horos was placed upon land that had been bought with the help of a loan. If the loan was not repaid, then the lender could take the farmer into slavery and also take possession of the land. When Solon canceled the debts, it would be natural to remove the stone giving evidence of the loan. Solon effectively made the land obtained through a loan fully the property of the borrower. This would explain what Solon meant in his poem. However, the first evidence for the use of the word "horos" to mean "mortgage stone" is not until 364 BC, well more than 200 years after Solon was archon. In addition, archaeologists have not uncovered any stone inscribed with mortgage agreements from before this later date.

So it remains unclear what Solon was doing when he pulled up the horoi. However, one other possibility exists. Perhaps the removal of the horoi is related to the return of those who had gone abroad as slaves or exiles. If an aristocrat had taken the land, he would have extended his own boundary markers to show this fact. When the former owners returned to their land, they would have wanted only their own markers on it. If it was considered wrong for the original owner to lose the land because of debt, then there would be no problem in pulling up the wrongfully planted horoi. Just as the original owner had been unjustly enslaved, the land had been made a slave to someone who was not its rightful owner.

As a further part of the seisachtheia, Solon abolished the class of hektemoroi (tenant farmers). As noted earlier, historians are unsure about the specifics of the hektemoroi. By the time the Athenians wrote about them, the hektemoroi were long gone, and no one could remember exactly what their position had been. If, as seems likely, they had become hektemoroi because of debt, the cancellation of debts would have removed their obligations to the landowners. Quite possibly Solon also gave them the land on which they worked (it may well have belonged to them originally in any case). In addition to changing the status of those who were hektemoroi in 594 BC, Solon

A Greek vase showing two warriors in hand-to-hand combat

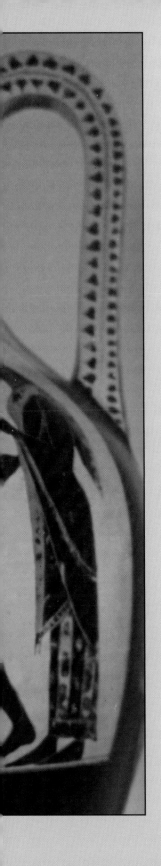

also changed the system so that people could no longer become hektemoroi in the future.

Clearly, the seisachtheia had a major impact on the lives of most Athenians. Those who were poor had a chance at a fresh start in life. Those who were wealthy lost out. No doubt some of them lost huge amounts, both in terms of land and of slaves. The gap between rich and poor had been reduced, at least for a time, and Solon must have felt that this would help to stop the crisis that was threatening the stability of the state.

THE CLASS SYSTEM

While the seisachtheia helped to make life better for the peasant farmers, it would not have made much difference to the newly rich. What they wanted was a share of power. Before Solon's reign, the aristocrats had kept the magistracies for themselves. In order for Solon to open up the magistracies to non-aristocrats, he had to change the qualifications for election. Previously, aristocratic birth had been required. This was why the newly rich could not get into office no matter how rich they became. They simply could not change the fact that they were not of noble birth. So Solon divided the people of Athens into four classes based on property: the *pentakosiomedimnoi* ("five hundred bushellers"), the *hippeis* ("horsemen"), the *zeugitae* ("yokemen"), and the *thetes* ("day laborers"). It is likely that the last three classes already existed in some form and that Solon simply organized them more effectively. These three groups relate to military service, since the hippeis could afford horses to ride into battle, the zeugitae could pay for armor to fight on foot, and the thetes were too poor to buy any armor. Solon probably created the pentakosiomedimnoi as a new class, as the name has no antecedents in the Greek language. It is possible that the word already existed and meant something quite general, like our word "millionaire." All of this applied only to the free Athenians. Slaves had no rights and were not even regarded as Athenians.

A painting of cloth merchants at work weighing bales of cloth

What Solon did was to specify exactly what official positions and rights each group should have. This was what allowed the newly rich to break through into positions of power. Solon enacted a law stating that the pentakosiomedimnoi were eligible for the position of archon and other official posts. The lesser magistracies were opened to the hippeis. Most important, Solon made membership in each class dependent on wealth, not birth. If the newly rich were wealthy enough to be pentakosiomedimnoi, they could also be elected archon, or one of the magistrates, giving them a share of power. However, the fact that the newly rich were eligible for election did not guarantee that they would be elected because the electors were still the members of the Areopagus, the council of aristocrats. No doubt a few of the newly rich were popular enough (or hosted good enough parties) that they were elected. Also, it is possible that aristocratic families had to marry their sons to the daughters of the newly rich to bring extra wealth into their families, which would have created political alliances. To ensure that the rest of the newly rich were not excluded from power, Solon changed the Areopagus so that its members were those who had held one of the nine official positions just below the archon. These officials became life members of the Areopagus. As the newly rich were occasionally elected, their influence gradually increased because after their year in office they became electors themselves.

Some doubt exists regarding exactly how the different property classes were organized. The name of the pentakosiomedimnoi means those with five hundred *medimnoi* (singular: medimnos). A medimnos was a Greek measure of capacity, roughly equal to eight gallons, or a bushel, hence the name is often translated "five hundred bushellers." This class, at least, is clear enough. Solon picked out those whose farms produced a large quantity of grain each year as being rich enough to be suitable to help govern the polis. Five hundred medimnoi of barley equate to about sixteen tons, which is enough to feed more than eighty people for a year. This figure, however, does not provide a full picture of the productivity of such farms. For example, additional produce was not measured by the medimnos—wine, olive oil, and livestock—and did not therefore count toward the assessment. In this era, no machines were available to help do the work, and so this level of production implies

A sixth-century BC clay tablet showing a potter at his wheel

very large farms and a great deal of wealth.

In ancient times, it was believed that Solon also set levels of production for the other classes: 300 medimnoi for the hippeis, and 200 bushels for the zeugitae. All those whose land produced less than 200 medimnoi of grain, or who had no land at all, were classified as thetes. It seems quite likely that later writers invented these levels of production and that Solon never actually applied them. Such levels imply a degree of wealth that was very high. If these quotas existed, many of those in the previous class of zeugitae would not have qualified to stay in their class and would have become thetes. As such, they would have had fewer rights under Solon than they previously had, which seems unlikely.

It is also difficult to see how each farmer would have been assessed, since there was no census or bureau of taxation with the kind of records required. It is most likely that the hippeis and zeugitae were still assessed in terms of their ability to provide the weapons and equipment of cavalry and infantry respectively. Their equipment provided visible evidence to which class they belonged, so no one would be in any doubt. Similarly, it must have been clear who produced enough from their farms to be counted as pentakosiomedimnoi simply by observing their lifestyles. If a dispute arose at any time, then it would be possible for the appropriate magistrate to make a more formal assessment, but this must have been the exception rather than the rule. Certainly a regular assessment of all Athenians would have been out of the question.

The thetes had only basic rights, and they were those Athenians who worked as hired laborers or perhaps had small market stalls. Without ownership of land, their opportunities were limited.

LEGAL REFORMS

Solon had removed the immediate threat of a crisis with the seisachtheia and his reform of the constitution to allow the newly rich access to

power. But he also realized that Athenian society needed further reform to avoid problems that might

A sculpture from the time of Solon of the multiheaded monster known as Typhon, whose body is that of a dragon. Zeus overcame Typhon with his thunderbolts.

arise in the future. What Athens needed was *eunomia*, the principle of "good order," through the law. As he said in a poem:

> Laws which are equal for peasant and noble
>
> Providing fair justice to each I wrote.

The Athenians remembered Solon most of all for his role as a lawgiver. More important, for the first time in Athenian history, Solon had all the nomoi written down. The nomoi changed from customs to laws. Instead of magistrates deciding legal cases on the basis of their own opinions and what had customarily been done in the past, Solon's reforms required officials to follow the law as it existed in written form for all citizens to see. This change from unwritten to written laws was vital for personal freedom. For the first time it was possible to check if what a magistrate decided was fair. Not only could justice be done, Athenians could see it being done.

Solon must have recorded all the nomoi that he knew and also spoke to other magistrates to find out what they thought the nomoi were in the past. Then he would have compared what he had put together with all the decisions that magistrates had recorded in previous years. Some of the nomoi would have been applied consistently, but others must have been used very inconsistently. Solon had to decide the fairest way to record each nomos so that it became an unchangeable law. Most likely, the nomoi of Drakon were probably not written down, or only a selected few were. Solon was the first to write down all the nomoi.

Not only did Solon record the nomoi as laws, he had them posted in the marketplace where people could see them. Everyone had the chance to find out exactly what the law said before appearing in a court. Everyone could tell if the magistrate was applying the law correctly. Instead of being controlled and kept secret by aristocrats, the law became public property.

However, it was no use knowing that a magistrate was not applying the law correctly if nothing could be done about it. So Solon introduced the right of appeal. This was the best way to protect the peasants from the aristocrats. To make the protection even better, Solon ordered that appeals be heard by a court of all adult male Athenians. This popular court was called the Heliaia. Every adult male Athenian was allowed to take part in hearings, and decisions were made by a vote. This meant that even the lowest class, the thetes, could take part in running Athens. If the peasants felt threatened by the decision of a magistrate, they could turn out in force and defeat it.

Together, the written laws and the right of appeal made the whole Athenian legal system much fairer. It was not perfect, however. Not all Athenians would have been well enough educated or literate enough to interpret the laws properly. And not all Athenians would have had the confidence to stand up in front

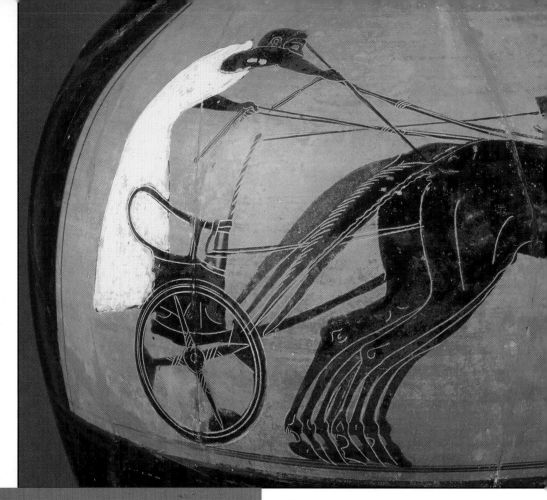

A vase painting depicting a Greek chariot

of a magistrate, or even the Heliaia (which could be thousands strong), and argue their cases. Solon could do little about illiteracy, since there was no state education system in Athens and no resources to provide one even if he had wanted to do this. But Solon tackled the problem of citizens feeling intimidated as he changed the law so that anyone could bring a charge against someone who was suspected of a crime. Previously, only the person who was the victim of the crime or a close family

member could bring charges, and it was the person who brought the charges who had to stand up in court. By allowing anyone to bring charges, Solon took the first step toward the creation of professional lawyers who could fight a case on someone else's behalf.

In practice, this change would have helped aristocrats to bring political charges against their enemies by pretending to support another person. It would have had to be a very serious crime for peasants to persuade someone else to take the time and trouble to fight cases for them. However, the principle was established, and it made justice a little more accessible for those in the lower class of society.

It is unknown today how many of the laws that later Athenians believed originated with Solon were actually his, but many probably were. One in particular, the law forbidding loans secured by a person's freedom, was definitely his. This meant that it was no longer possible for someone who could not repay a loan to be enslaved. This protected the peasants from sinking back into the kind of financial problems and debt that had made the seisachtheia necessary. Conversely, it meant that the very poor might have nothing at all to offer as a guarantee that they would repay loans, making it impossible for them to borrow money to improve their situations in life.

One other law, usually credited to Solon, allowed property to be willed to someone who was not a blood relative. If someone had no sons to inherit his property (and only men could own property at that time), he was allowed in his will to adopt someone from outside the family as a son. This newly created heir would then inherit and continue the family line.

Many examples of laws attributed to Solon, but probably not his creations, could be given. A man could kill an adulterer without fear of punishment. A woman caught committing adultery was forbidden to wear jewelry and could have any punishment other than mutilation or death inflicted upon her. Drunkenness in a magistrate was punishable by death. At night, a thief could be killed instantly; in the day, he had to be taken before the court. It was forbidden to speak ill of the dead. All these were genuine Athenian laws, but it is unlikely that Solon created them. Either they were older nomoi that Solon wrote down, or they were added to the list later. One of the problems historians face is that after the nomoi were recorded and displayed in public, new laws were simply added at the end of Solon's list. It was quickly forgotten that they were not there originally, and so after a few years any law on the public list was thought to be part of the laws of Solon.

ECONOMIC REFORMS

The Athenians believed that Solon carried out a number of economic reforms, and it is possible that this was the case. Some laws relating to farming were attributed to Solon, such as the rule that trees had to be planted at least five feet from a neighbor's land, and that beehives had to be at least 300 feet from a neighbor's hives. But historians do not specifically know the origin of these laws.

However, historians today do believe that Solon was genuinely responsible for certain reforms, including a temporary prohibition on

A fifth-century BC vase painting of Greek hoplites, or infantrymen, putting on their armor

the export of farm produce apart from olive oil, and a law granting citizenship to skilled foreign craftsmen who immigrated to Athens. The latter measure encouraged the development of small-scale industries and trade in finished products. The former measure would have prevented aristocrats from using their surplus grain to obtain luxuries, and it would have kept more grain in Attica, thus keeping the price down so that the peasants could afford it. The only product that Attica had too much of was olive oil, so this was excluded from the ban. Grain (usually barley), olives, and grapes were the staple crops. Most Athenians would have lived on a diet of barley, olives, fish, wine, and cheese (from goat's milk). Few could afford to eat meat except on special occasions. Olive oil could be used for many purposes, from cooking oil to fuel for lamps.

Soon after the time of Solon, Athens began to surpass the polis of Corinth as the place where the best Greek pottery was produced. This may have been a coincidence, but it does suggest that Solon had made life easier for foreign craftsmen. However, no evidence exists to support the idea that a shortage of grain occurred in Attica at the time of Solon.

However, there clearly was such a shortage in the fifth century BC, so the export ban may well not be genuine. Most Greek poleis were normally more or less self-sufficient in their food requirements.

Solon also changed the Athenian system of weights and measures. Up until Solon's time, Athens had used the Aeginetan system, but Solon changed to the Euboic standard. In the Aeginetan system, a drachma (the basic unit of currency) equaled about six and one-third grams of silver. Under the Euboic standard, the drachma equaled four and one-quarter grams of silver. Because most of the principal trading poleis of Greece used the Euboic standard, this change allowed Athens to trade and compete with them more easily, strengthening the Athenian economy. The ancient writers believed that Solon changed the coinage at the same time, or even issued the first Athenian coins. Modern archaeology shows that this cannot have been the case. As noted previously, the earliest Athenian coins date to about 575 BC, some twenty years after Solon was archon. Nevertheless, with these other economic reforms, Athens would have been in a better position to take advantage of coins when they were introduced.

AFTER THE REFORMS

Solon believed that with the seisachtheia, the new system of classes, and the written laws he had put forth, Athens had a chance at eunomia (good order). He claimed that:

> To the people I have given as much as they deserve,
> Neither taking away their rights nor giving too much.
> Those who had power and were admired for their wealth,
> I have made sure they suffered no indignity.
> I have stood with a strong shield flung around both sides,
> And not allowed either an unfair victory.

But some Athenians, those whose privileges were now restricted, thought that Solon's reforms had cost them too much, and they complained bitterly. A fragment of one of Solon's poems reads:

> In great works to please everyone is difficult.

Elsewhere Solon wrote:

> Everyone thought they would make a
>   fortune. . .
> . . . and now they are angry with me,
> And all give me sideways glances as if I
>   were an enemy.

According to the legends, Solon left Athens for ten years, having made a law that no one could change any part of what he had done without his agreement. It is not known what Solon did on these travels. Perhaps he went back to being a merchant, or maybe he simply enjoyed traveling. Most important, he wanted to avoid Athenians asking him questions about his reforms. They had to take their own responsibility for making the reforms work.

Solon traveled around the Mediterranean, probably visiting Egypt and Cyprus, before returning to Athens. One famous story tells how he visited the court of Croesus, king of Lydia, an area of modern Turkey. Croesus was famous for his wealth. Today, people still talk about someone being "as rich as Croesus." He boasted to Solon that he was the happiest man alive. Solon replied that people should not be considered to have had happy lives until after they die because life can always turn sour. Solon was right. Croesus eventually lost everything. Since Solon probably died before Croesus came to the throne of Lydia, the story is unlikely to be true.

ATHENS AFTER SOLON

Although Solon reformed the constitution, he could not control what the Athenians did with their new rights. Life was better for the poorest Athenians, but the aristocrats were still behaving arrogantly and competing for power. Because of aristocratic rivalries, the Areopagus was unable to agree on an archon in 590 BC and in 586 BC. The archon chosen for 581 BC, Damisas, refused to stand down from office at the end of his year and held onto power for an extra ten months before being removed. Less than fifteen years after Solon's reforms, it was clear that although the reforms had prevented a mass revolution, they could not protect Athens against ambitious individuals seeking power.

It was not long before what the aristocrats feared most actually

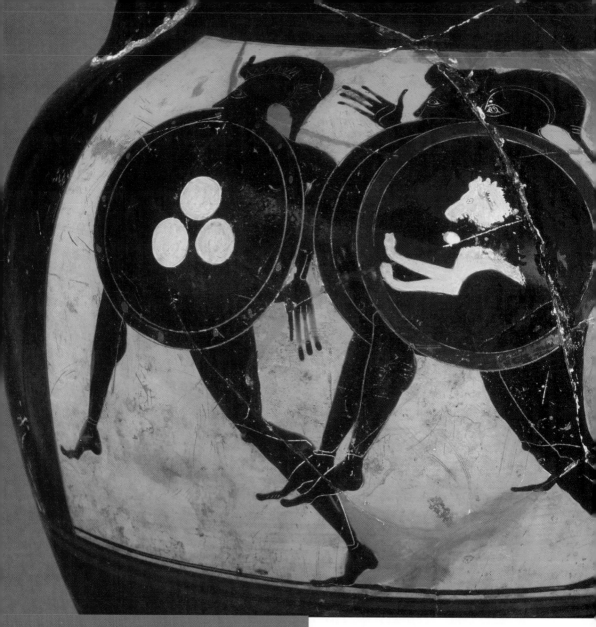

A vase painting of armed runners from the Panathenaea, one of four annual Athenian festivals and athletic tournaments

happened. A prominent aristocrat called Peisistratos, who had been a successful polemarch in the war against Megara, attempted to become tyrant. In 561 BC, Peisistratos entered the marketplace in Athens after inflicting wounds upon himself. He

claimed that political enemies had attacked him, and the Athenians gave him a body-guard, which he then used to take control of the Acropolis. The supporters of two other aristocrats, Lykourgos and Megakles, managed to drive Peisistratos out of Athens. Megakles was the grandson of the earlier Megakles, who expelled Kylon.

A few years later, circa 557 BC, Peisistratos tried again. This time his trick was even more daring. He found a beautiful, six-foot-tall woman called Phye, and he dressed her as the goddess Athena. He started a rumor that the goddess was bringing him back to Athens personally and drove into Athens on a chariot, with Phye beside him. This time Peisistratos had the support of Megakles, whose daughter he was to marry. The Athenians were completely fooled, and Peisistratos established himself as tyrant. However, the marriage of Peisistratos and

A Greek vase painting of a wrestling match

Megakles' daughter was not happy, and when she complained to her father, he withdrew his support of Peisistratos, who was once more forced to leave Athens.

Peisistratos tried to assume power a third time. He raised a good deal of money and gathered together troops with the help of his friends in other poleis. After a ten-year absence, in 546 BC, he arrived in Attica at the head of an army. There was little resistance, and his position as tyrant was secure. This time it was Megakles who had to leave Athens. Peisistratos ruled Athens until his death in 527 BC. Although he did not officially change the laws or any of the constitutional arrangements of Solon, he did add some new measures of his own, and some of the old laws must have gone out of use. It was at this time that the confusion over which laws were genuinely enacted by Solon began to grow.

After the death of Peisistratos, his son Hippias took over as tyrant. Where Peisistratos had been popular, reducing the power of the aristocracy and building many fine temples in Athens, Hippias was very unpopular, and his regime became brutal and violent. An assassination attempt in 514 BC only managed to kill Hipparkhos, the brother of Hippias. In the end, it required the intervention of Sparta, one of the leading poleis in Greece, to remove Hippias from power in 510 BC.

The Athenians were determined never to endure the rule of a tyrant again. When Cleisthenes came forward in 508 BC with a plan to change the constitution, he won great support. Cleisthenes radically changed the political system in Athens. He gave ultimate power to the Ekklesia, an assembly of all male adult Athenian citizens, and set up an executive council to advise the Ekklesia. All members of the assembly could speak and vote in the Ekklesia and could be chosen by lot to serve for one year on the executive council. The right to become magistrates was extended to hippeis and zeugitae, and in practice the thetes were never excluded either. This was power exercised by the people and for the people. Athens had become a democracy. The Athenians did not at this time call their system *demokratia* ("people power"); they called it *isonomia* or "equality in law," something that would not have been possible without Solon's reforms. Cleisthenes did not attempt to make changes to the laws, many of which were still those that Solon had first written down.

WHAT WE OWE SOLON

Solon did not create a democracy in Athens. He was not even trying to do so, as his poetry reveals:

> The people will best follow their leaders,
> If they are neither too free nor too
>   restricted.

Solon remained an aristocrat at heart and wanted to avoid the overthrow of the ruling class through popular discontent. However, he also worked on the principle of fairness. Solon saw that it was unfair for the poor Athenians who worked hard for the good of the polis to be enslaved, and so he gave them freedom. He saw that it was unfair for those who worked hard to be deprived of political rights, and so he gave them their chance by changing from a system based on birth to one based on wealth. Solon thought it was fair that those who owned most of the land and wealth should have control over that land and wealth, so he left power in the hands of the rich. He also realized that it was fair for the poor to be free from exploitation, so he wrote down the laws to protect them.

A fragment of pottery showing a sixth-century BC Greek galley

The principle of the rule of law is central to any democracy. It means that members of the democracy can know and enforce their rights. The rule of law means that the laws overrule the will of any individual leader and that the leader must obey the laws as much as any other citizen. Solon established the rule of law at Athens with his eunomia.

Although Solon achieved his short-term goal of avoiding an immediate political crisis, in the long term his reforms were a failure because the established order was overthrown when Peisistratos became tyrant of Athens.

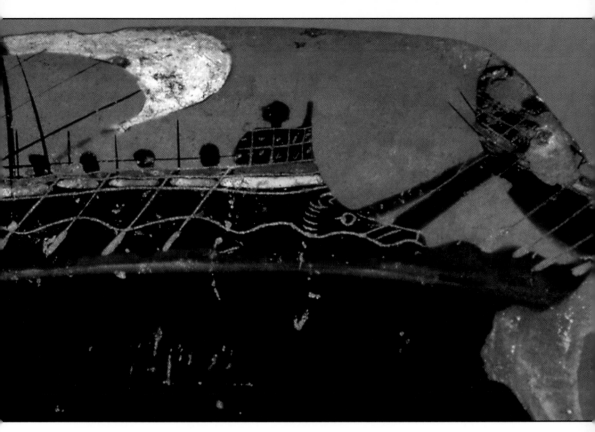

However, by the fourth century BC, the Athenians remembered Solon as the Father of Democracy because they still had the laws he had written down. They also knew that he had given freedom to the poorest Athenians, which was a necessary first step before Cleisthenes gave them political rights.

Some nations today have democratic political systems because the Athenians had one. When people during the Renaissance studied the literature and philosophy of the Athenians, they also studied the Athenian political system, and that system was democracy. Just as intellectuals tried to copy the literature, they also aimed to imitate the political system, and this gave rise to modern democracy. Solon made Athenian democracy possible, and so he also made later democracies possible, including that of the United States. Portraits of Solon are displayed in the U.S. Supreme Court and the U.S. House of Representatives.

THE PROBLEM OF EVIDENCE

As discussed throughout this book, few precise details are known about Solon. Even when a fact is known, it can often have many interpretations or its significance is not fully understood. This is because when Solon was alive no one wrote down the events that happened during his reign, or if someone did, that record is lost. The very first known book about history was not written until about 530 BC. After this time, the Athenians did try to write about the life and times of Solon, but they did not have a written record of what he had done. They had some pieces of the poems attributed to Solon, they had some laws that Solon was credited with enacting, and they had oral traditions, stories passed on from parents to children.

The problem with oral traditions is that although they can be very reliable, there is also the risk that the storyteller wants to embellish

A Greek vase painting of a hunter

the story. By the time a story has been passed down through a couple of generations, it is sometimes impossible to say which parts of the story are true and which are made up. So when the Athenians finally wrote about Solon, it was as if they had only half the pieces of a jigsaw puzzle. But they did their best to make sense of what they knew and to imagine what the whole picture would have looked like.

Today, only a few of the books that the ancient Athenians wrote survive. Whereas the earlier Athenians could look at dozens of poems and choose which ones to quote, modern historians have only the lines of poetry recorded in those later works. The ancients could look at all the laws that Solon was said to have made and choose the ones they thought were genuine. Contemporary scholars have only the laws the ancients selected. And the same is true of the oral tradition. If the early Athenians who followed Solon got it wrong, then there is little chance today that we can be confident of getting it right. It is clear that the ancients did not always get it right, because sometimes they disagreed with each other. At other times, it is clear that they were only guessing, because what they said was deliberately vague.

Of the many books that the Greeks wrote about Solon, only two have survived. One, known as the *Constitution of Athens*, was written by Aristotle in about 335 BC. Aristotle was a philosopher who was interested in how human society worked. He collected information about many different Greek poleis, one of which was Athens. Because he was writing about the history of the constitution of Athens, he would have tried to get information that was as accurate as possible. However, since the book is not just about Solon, the section devoted to his achievements is not very detailed.

The other book is the *Life of Solon* by Plutarch, written about AD 100, which is about 700 years after the events he describes. Just think about how much historians now disagree about explorer Christopher Columbus, who lived just 500 years ago, in an age of written records. Because it was written so long after Solon, the book is much more confusing than the *Constitution of Athens* by Aristotle. It has much more information, however. It also describes Solon himself, not just what he did. The problem is that most of the stories Plutarch provides about Solon are from the oral tradition and are not reliable.

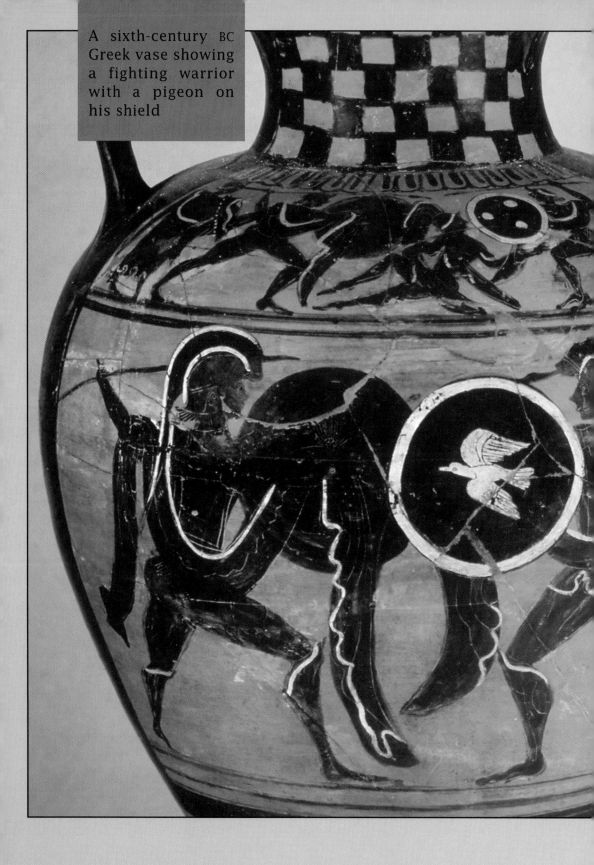

A sixth-century BC Greek vase showing a fighting warrior with a pigeon on his shield

These two writers cite many quotations from the poems of Solon. There are also many other writers who quoted from Solon's poems, even if they were not writing about Solon himself. Some of these include lawyers who wrote down the speeches they made in court to help train their students. Because Solon wrote many of the laws of Athens, he is sometimes mentioned.

Today, when historians try to sort out what Solon really did and what is simply fiction, they compare all the different pieces of information available. For example, sometimes one ancient writer tells a story about Solon and a different ancient writer tells the exact story about someone else. This often means that the story is true about the person who lived first, although sometimes it is clearly not true about either. For example, the ancient writers believed that Solon changed the coins of Athens. But archaeology tells us that Athens

did not have coins until after Solon was archon, so he cannot have changed them.

By testing evidence in this way, historians can create theories about what is presumed to be true. Unfortunately, there is no guarantee that the details are correct. Sometimes it is simply a guess.

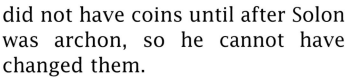

A painting on the inside of an ancient Greek drinking bowl showing Achilles dressing the wounds of Patroclus. Achilles and Patroclus were legendary heroes of the Trojan War.

GLOSSARY

acropolis "High city." The Greeks built most of their cities on or around a hill, which was called an acropolis. This hill was easy to defend from enemies, and if anyone attacked, the people of the city would retreat to it. The most important temples were also located on the acropolis. The most famous acropolis in Greece is the one in Athens (often simply known as the Acropolis).

archon This word could mean anyone who was in charge of something, but usually it means someone with an official government position. At Athens, the most senior magistrate was called the archon.

Areopagus "Hill of Ares." A small hill in Athens, sacred to Ares, the god of war, where the aristocratic council met. More commonly used as the name of the council itself.

Aristotle The Greek philosopher who wrote a description of the Athenian political system under Solon around 335 BC.

Attica The name given to the geographical region surrounding the polis of Athens.

demokratia "People power." The system of direct rule of a polis by all the citizens, meeting in the Ekklesia.

Ekklesia The name of the assembly of all citizens at Athens, which met for one day approximately forty times each year to decide policies and to pass laws. Cleisthenes gave it these powers, although it may have existed in a limited form earlier.

eunomia The principle that stated that society should be balanced, with no one group having more power than they deserved. It corresponds to the modern idea of the rule of law.

gods The Greeks believed in many gods and goddesses, the most important of whom was Zeus, the father of the gods. The Greeks believed that each god was responsible for particular aspects of nature or human activity. Athena was the goddess of cities.

hektemoroi "Sixth-parters." A group of Athenians who worked on farms for one-sixth of what they produced.

Heliaia The name given to the court of all adult male Athenians, which Solon established to hear appeals against the decisions of magistrates.

hippeis "Horsemen." The name of the second of Solon's classes, whose land produced enough for them to be able to maintain a horse and fight in the cavalry.

horoi [horos] Marker stones. The Greeks did not use fences to mark their land, instead they would use freestanding stones inscribed with the name of the owner of the land. Sometimes there was other information, such as whether the land had been sold or had been paid for with a loan. Horoi are sometimes also known as boundary stones. As boundary markers, they were believed to be under the protection of Zeus, the supreme god.

isonomia The principle that stated that all citizens had a right to equal treatment under the law.

magistrate An individual with an official government position (called a magistracy), who had legal powers to act as a judge and, to some extent, to make new laws. Different magistrates would deal with different areas of law (for example, business contracts or marriage).

medimnos [medimnoi] A Greek measure of capacity, roughly equal to eight gallons or the modern bushel. It was used to measure dry produce such as grain or flour.

nomoi [nomos] The same Greek word means both unwritten customs and written laws. It was possible to win a case in court by appealing to tradition, especially if it was a religious tradition.

Olympic Games The Greeks started the Olympic Games in 776 BC at Olympia in southern Greece (not the same place as Mount Olympus in northern Greece where the gods were believed to live). The games were held every four years, and only men were allowed to take part. The events were track and field, chariot races, wrestling, and boxing. The only prize was for the athlete who came first. The winner received a wreath of olive leaves. Athletes' home cities treated them as celebrities.

oracle The name given to any of the places where the Greeks believed they could go and get advice directly from the gods, and also the term used for the piece of advice given. The most famous (and supposedly most reliable) was the oracle at Delphi (known as the Delphic Oracle). The Greeks believed that when the Delphic priestess of Apollo (god of prophecy) went into a trance, the god spoke through her. People would ask questions about the future or ask for help in solving problems they were experiencing.

Plutarch A roman historian who wrote a biography of Solon some time around 100 AD.

polemarch The title of the magistrate at Athens who was responsible for the army.

polis [poleis] The name for a Greek city-state. Many Greek cities had only a few thousand inhabitants and ruled as little as fifty square miles.

sanctuary The area surrounding every Greek temple. A wall marked the sanctuary. People who had committed a crime could go to a temple and claim sanctuary. They were safe from arrest as long as they remained in the sanctuary area.

seisachtheia "Shaking off of burdens." The name of Solon's cancellation of debts, which included setting debt-slaves free and abolishing hektemoroi.

Thales of Miletus One of the earliest of the Greek philosophers, who insisted that explanations of phenomena should be based on empirical or logical principles rather than on religious ideas.

thetes Day laborers. The lowest of Solon's classes, including all those who were too poor to possess their own pair of oxen. This would include those with very small farms or with no land at all.

tyrant Someone who took power in a polis by force and ruled as an individual. The newly rich often supported tyrants. They were usually popular because they reduced the power of the aristocracy and treated everyone equally. Although some were ruthless and violent, others genuinely cared for the people they ruled. For the Greeks, the word "tyrant" did not imply a bad person.

zeugitae "Yokemen." The third of Solon's classes, whose land produced enough for them to keep a pair of oxen of their own (the yoke allows oxen to pull a plough). They would be wealthy enough to pay for the armor to fight in the infantry.

FOR MORE INFORMATION

American Classical League
Miami University
Oxford, OH 45056
e-mail: info@aclclassics.org
Web site: http://www.aclclassics.org

The Classical Association
Room 323, Third Floor
Senate House, Malet Street
London WC1E 7HU
United Kingdom
+44-020-7862-8706
e-mail: croberts@sas.ac.uk
Web site: http://www.sas.ac.uk/icls/
   classass

International Plutarch Society
Department of History
Utah State University
Old Main Building, Room 323
Logan, UT 84322-0710
Web site: http://www.usu.edu/history/
   plout.htm

National Junior Classical League
Miami University
Oxford, OH 45056-1694
(513) 529-7741
Web site: http://www.njcl.org

WEB SITES

Due to the changing nature of Internet links, the Rosen Publishing Group, Inc., has developed an online list of Web sites related to the subject of this book. This site is updated regularly. Please use this link to access the list:

http://www.rosenlinks.com/lag/solo/

FOR FURTHER READING

Altman, Susan, and Susan Lechner. *Ancient Greece*. New York: Children's Press, 2001.

Amos, H. D., and A. G. P. Lang. *These Were the Greeks*. New York: Dufour Editions, 1997.

Bains, Rae. *Ancient Greece*. Mahwah, NJ: Troll Associates, 1985.

Bardi, Matilde. *Ancient Greece*. New York: Bedrick Books, 2000.

Cartledge, Paul, ed. *The Cambridge Illustrated History of Ancient Greece*. New York: Cambridge University Press, 1998.

Howatson, Margaret, ed. *The Oxford Companion to Classical Literature*. Oxford, England: Oxford University Press, 1989.

Murray, Oswyn. *Early Greece*. Cambridge, MA: Harvard University Press, 1993.

BIBLIOGRAPHY

Copeland, Tim. *Ancient Greece.* New York: Cambridge University Press, 1997.

Dunstan, William. *Ancient Greece.* Fort Worth, TX: Harcourt College Publishers, 2000.

Freeman, Kathleen. *The Work and Life of Solon.* New York: Arno Press, 1976.

Mitchell, Lynette, and Peter Rhodes. *The Development of the Polis in Archaic Greece.* London: Routledge, 1997.

Thiel, Johannes Hendrik. *Studies in Ancient History.* Amsterdam: J. C. Gieben, 1994.

Woodhouse, W. *Solon the Liberator.* London: Oxford University Press, 1938.

INDEX

ABOUT THE AUTHOR

Bernard Randall read ancient history and philosophy at St. Andrew's University, Scotland, before moving to the University of Edinburgh for a master's degree in classics. He is shortly to complete his doctorate on fifth-century BC Greece at the University of Manchester. His main research interest is the history of Sparta up to 400 BC. His other interests include early church history, theology, rugby, and juggling.

CREDITS

PHOTO CREDITS

Cover, pp. 42–43, 55 © AKG London/John Hios; cover inset, p. 3 © Scala/Art Resource; p. 8 © Werner Forman Archive/National Museum, Athens; pp. 12–13, 20–21, 36, 40, 44–45, 48, 61, 64–65, 70–71, 82–83, 84, 88–89, 91, 94–95 © AKG London/Eric Lessing; pp. 14–15, 46, 96–97 © AKG Photo; pp. 16–17, 22–23, 32 © Werner Forman Archive; pp. 26–27, 52–53, 74–75 © AKG London/Peter Connolly; p. 38 © The Art Archive/National Museum Athens/Dagli Orti; pp. 58–59 © AKG London; p. 67 © Werner Forman Archive/Acropolis Museum, Athens.

SOLON: THE LAWMAKER OF ATHENS

EDITOR

Jake Goldberg

DESIGN

Evelyn Horovicz

LAYOUT

Hillary Arnold